PULLEYS & LOCOMOTION

Black Lawrence Press
www.blacklawrence.com

Executive Editor and Art Director: Colleen Ryor
Managing Editor: Diane Goettel
Book Design: Steven Seighman and Colleen Ryor

Copyright © 2009 Rachel Galvin

All rights reserved. Except for brief quotations in critical articles or reviews, no part of this book may be reproduced in any manner without prior written permission from the publisher:

Black Lawrence Press
8405 Bay Parkway C8
Brooklyn, N.Y. 11214
U.S.A.

Published 2009 by Black Lawrence Press, a division of Dzanc Books

Cover Image: Francis Picabia, "Parade Amoureuse," 1917
© 2009 Artists Rights Society (ARS), New York / ADAGP, Paris

First edition 2009

Printed in the United States

PULLEYS
&
LOCOMOTION

poems

Rachel
Galvin

Black Lawrence Press
New York

TABLE OF CONTENTS

7   *Consult these photographs...*

9   Village of Pulleys & Locomotion

10   The Baker Folds What He Does Not Remember

11   In Cambium Lucida

12   Looking for Hibiscus

13   Trains Pass, Close But Invisible

15   *Enter the region from the northwest...*

17   Village of Twice-Salted Seas

18   When the Vision Comes, the Eye's Engine Will Sequence Clarity

23   After the Eclipse: Village Tale

24   Tzimtzum

25   After the Eclipse: Village Riddle

26   Traveling Peddler's Declaration

27   *The celebrated composer Kadison...*

29   Both Members of This Club

32   How to Build Your Own Zoetrope

33   Limber at Full Speed

34 Flammable Letter

35 *So that birds of prey may easily...*

37 Scenic Overlook One Hundred Yards

38 Interlude in the Insomniac Village

39 When All Speech Has Ceased Within

41 Letter Spoken in Wind

43 *As if with pollen, Jerusalem...*

44 Invitations to the God

45 Gematria

46 Squire the Hour

47 The *Dulce*

50 Letter as an Ode

51 Eros

53 *River View of the Village*

54 In Gaitskill Bog

55 Quietus

59 As Light Breaks

60 Détrompe l'Oeil

61 Pilgrim Road

Consult these photographs as you tour the region.

1. I walk in a crowd of umbrellas, where women display green parkas and wool scarves for sale, offer varieties of the sea. I purchase a zoetrope cut from onionskin. Its label reads *flammable*.

2. Hovering by my ear—*mein dybbuk*—a strange light latches to my shoulder.

3. I keep a knot of amber under my tongue as I set out to wake the noon sun.

Village of Pulleys & Locomotion

I trail my suitcase along the platform,
the weight of the air
at the small of my back.

A man used to arrive from afar,
give each child a whistle, and parade them
through the village, whistling.

What is this fury of forms, boarding
trains, handing out whistles to children?
Dear rubber valve, dear spigot—if

this world is the only world,
Anaximander will go on shaking his sieve,
persistently sifting with an ear to the ignition—

striker of matches, your scent of cloves, your fire
rides the circumference and gyrates at the center.
There is the vermiform signature: *you may eat*

of this tree. Now the glorious propinquity, now
the rupture. A village elder goes on debating
with his god. Who can tell if he receives a reply?

In the old stories, if you whistled,
the light would come to you
out of curiosity.

The Baker Folds What He Does Not Remember

with eggs into each bowl of batter,
brushes it over bread—his kitchen
emits the sweet tenor of yeast. He rises
early to bake day's first loaves,
his window a yellow square
in the alley: where the city turns,
and turns again, ensemble of sugar,
flour, cream. A woman comes for
the kitchen scent, stands by the back door.
When he rolls his sleeves above his elbows,
she sees *my mother's soul* written on one arm,
my father's soul written on the other.

In Cambium Lucida

Sweet calendula, is it true what the gardener said—
when we learn the name of a thing

we no longer see it? If only I might hear the cinctured sorrow
in the cilia, the rumor of upshoot.

Rain makes love in its own language, uttering a phrase
in recitative,

a conversation in formlessness. It has a strange elation, as waves do
coming to the shore,

the multiplicity of a fluid touched with the thousand ideas
of photosynthesis,

dark sugared tubes whose relation to light dilates, as the arborvitae
abandons shingles

and fence posts for totems and seafaring vessels, in all shapes
branching into the mutable.

Looking for Hibiscus

The front door was blue, now it is red.
My mother looks for her grandmother's

courtyard where she used to play. *Falling coconuts*
may shatter a windshield. It's only six blocks

to the ocean, so just slip on your
flip-flops. The back door is gone:

its outline has shifted four feet
to the left. A Russian wants to sell her

his car, an apartment right here
or down the block. Grandma Rose

the Volozhin anarchist used to walk here by herself
in Flamingo Park, which has no flamingos.

It's too hot for arguing, it will dehydrate you.
And for god's sake wear a hat. Even in the shade.

Trains Pass, Close But Invisible

But isn't concealment half of beauty?
The air's tremble as it ungloves
each finger, sets strands

of web to glint. The uplift of cedars,
free of gravitas, their vault
and nave unencumbered

by the unfinished business of the soul,
its shivering coastlines.
Nearby aspens ring their yellow bells,

hungry, uncertain how to spend their days.
But this may be a failure of the eye,
vertex of nerve sewn to world.

The yellow rustle may not be bells,
but a roomful of readers
turning pages of newspaper.

Enter the region from the northwest. Follow the lakeshore east until you reach the town's straightest avenue. Once an engine of industry, this sector has lagged for a decade. Now seagulls shell peas in parking lots. Follow the ridge that runs south. The winged building facing you was constructed from memory. At its summit, a turning restaurant scatters daylight along the river like salt.

Village of Twice-Salted Seas

I look up at my grandmother over the stew pot
she is stirring—in a dream of hornets,

I kneel on one unknowingly. It enters
my left knee. Standing on one leg, I recite

*She preferred salt on all her meals, she believed
the soul was finite, she loved noisily.*

*She whom the grocer hid in a barrel to escape the Cossacks.
She who used a broom to beat my father,*

*left her children in London, Ballyminton, Rochester.
She who raised her children Jews,*

*she who raised her children Catholics.
Who spoke Russian before English,*

*Yiddish before Russian before Hebrew,
who used different gestures in each language.*

*She who kept her letters in a soup tureen.
Told my father to fuck off one Christmas day.*

*Who ran anarchist meetings, who had a harelip,
who was left without a cow to live by.*

Mysterious kitchen, duty and dominion,
she covers her eyes with both hands,

carrots and prunes boiling together, phrases
of steam, seed-shaped consonants.

When the Vision Comes, the Eye's Engine Will Sequence Clarity

Inventive eye, that through this narrow slit
      joins world to world, my seat
to those adjacent, our rows dissolving
      in the dim theater, this peopled urgency.
News footage simulates the last century:

      a woman running shoeless in snow,
her inaudible voice. The screen is vacant
      more than half the time, yet the eye skips,
eager for narrative, arc of separation
      and reconciliation, green of actual day.

Eye and mind collude, I forget
      I sit in obscurity, breath held
as the heroine focuses binoculars—
      in this theater of distance

I blink binary into pulsation,
      hummingbird's thrum unaccounted,
static points of light smoothed
      into motion, suspension, nexus.

און איצט טייערע לייענער איז אייערע איבער צו דערציילן די מעשות אין אייערע אייגענע ווערטער.

And now, dear readers, it is your turn to retell these tales in your own words.

After the Eclipse: Village Tale

When we woke all flesh was blue.
The bell in the square, rescued from a Volozhin fire,
now Prussian blue, Chaya's oxen

a bright French blue, linens on the line
and the morning minyan's prayers
tinted from hyacinth to wisteria.

Overnight clocks had regained authority, took
metronomes for brides. Young Rivka stashed the last
unofficial green in a basket of apples and ran

to her Moishe, who in three minutes recounted
the original malady of every stone in the village.
Where to find a remedy? We fluttered

our hands in supplication, merchants went on conversing
in the marketplace, adding consonants on one hand,
launching sums on paper wings—

how the houses rose to resemble people!
There, like a handkerchief emerging
from the breast pocket of each villager, was the name.

Tzimtzum

Faith lies in the pleasure
of speculation, as wood requires oxygen
to burn: this soul wishes above all

to witness fire's consequences,
its emanations (wax, clay, sugar),
to solve, from all equations bundled,

for the genuine variable—apex—
mathesis singularis, a voice
issuing from a thicket. Kindling

the air the way red cedars
blaze into beacon, transforming
pigment back to element.

After the Eclipse: Village Riddle

The tzaddik arrived in a clamoring throng,
walking behind his carriage.
A tailor asked, *Why don't you ride?*

Hidden among the peacock-blue
chickens, the holy man convened a conference
of locksmiths' children. *Like a thief,*

you must be willing to risk your life
even for a small lock. Some muttered *lies.*
Others cheered, hoisted the chickens

in the air. As the tzaddik took his leave,
he saw that the folds between garden
and sea were patrolled by a goat,

a rooster, and a nude woman.
But who was the one clothed in wildflowers
who didn't wave farewell?

Traveling Peddler's Declaration

And why, and when, and who, strangers shout
from the open doorways. *And how, and how.* Each greets me
by name. I will take the blue ink and dip it in water
though it goes on staining, and the heart, in its endless cracking—
a tree aching for ground—can rest an hour.

The celebrated composer Kadison, whose name means rich and blessed man, lived here seven generations ago. His eldest son was taken during a pogrom, and not long after, the family home was destroyed in a conflagration—set by sparks from a neighbor's breakfast—that devastated the entire village but the bell in the main square. Kadison's daughter rebuilt this staircase to honor her father, and it has become a resting spot for travelers. Today one can contemplate the cast iron and brickwork at the site where Kadison would, in days past, devise melodies that told of the village's melancholy, the secret life of its yams and carrots.

Both Members of This Club
after George Bellows

In which the body curves in interrogation
to meet the divine full stop. Each leans all strength,

forehead presses to glass. An all-night
struggle as with a river to ford.

Endurance of the name charging forward
and back, running its course to climax

when the adversary, demon or reflection, strikes Jacob
with awe, pries his head back to see

the ladder—his face radiant with doubt—
he, the pale one, now disfigured, the indelible

traced onto his hip, his body's antiphony,
at the place where the river Yabbok

and the word *struggle* are of one root.
Here, all night, the question.

And after dawn, the new name, new limp,
all ballast tossed, still the question. And so,

unsure if he has prevailed,
he goes forth to find his brother.

> The universe is a fixed point.
> *Edmond Jabès*

How to Build Your Own Zoetrope

Rely on your eye for illusion of motion.
Today we will stride where yesterday
was only space: the crux of mechanic cinema.

These words, these apertures. Will later reveal
your handiwork. Do you see the waters withdraw?
Rely on your eye for illusion.

Fold the errant rim at right angles.
Renounce idolatry. This is crucial.
Confront the torso like a lamp.

What girandole, what éclat. Cleave
to the right angle. Rely on your eye.
Affix your story here: *Of lies and history.*

Figures move naturally at fourteen frames
per second and if you have pictured me,
at this rate I will always run toward you,

years hence, luminous, blurred
with expectation. Rely on it:
motion lies in the eye. The rest of us are still.

Limber at Full Speed

Between outset x and upheaval y:
that the girl will slip in seconds
does not erase the instant slid.
Bent as in utero, yet leaping,
arms extended, lips indigo,
she shoots the cresting water,
the propulsion not her own,
glittering tethered girl, and now:
and in day's darkening eye.
Tell me, André Kertész,
does the triangulation undo you
as it undoes me? What of the men
who roost on gravel? What candor
in the diagonal between stacked crates?
What hovers between one and two
of the clock's face? What flurry, this,
what supple approach of road?

Flammable Letter

He kneels by the bed:
a general in ceremonial dress,
holding his head on a tray.
A resigned expression,
watching me as I sleep.

So that birds of prey may easily ingest the corpse, speeding the reincarnation of flesh and breath in flesh, Tibetan Buddhists dismember their dead. Inside a locked mailbox, a letter. The wind bared its hem as I passed a butcher shop, pheasants and rabbits hung upside-down, inside-out. A release of rain filled the café with people. I discovered my heart had a seam like a walnut, you could press to lever it open and expose its dark, wet dividers.

Scenic Overlook One Hundred Yards

When he found a woman
who would rub his feet there was no further he would ride.

No hankering after motor and rev.
Only the tap of tiles laid one by the other. Her name

escapes me now, but the coffee rings remain. I am condemned
to the sudden sparrow, for this country is not symmetrical.

Wildlife swipes food in a gabble, immolates,
air saturates with goldfinches, luster of corposant.

At a roadside Park 'n Eat we spoke of what it takes
to unfurl a belief of this size. And maintain it.

I was convinced it was a buzz saw,
or something unzipped, but

it could have been the blue mountains
laying their wagers.

Interlude in the Insomniac Village

Daughter of unsynched clocks:
whose rooms will not remain
within the same minute—her family,

torn apart by sleeplessness, left her down the road
with empty dippers in each hand—*did she have two hearts,
circling each other like maddened moths?*

When All Speech Has Ceased Within

A woman in a red coat gazed at a photo of herself naked,
her hair tucked into a hat. If she impersonated herself

long enough, would she become what she saw?
When she retreats, language meets clay, space

smoothes into line. Who are the bearers of compassion,
my friend. She left, erasing the diagrams

of her thoughts as she went.
                              Your room of blue sand.

What if science, in flares of electric light, were scattered
through the centuries—aerial view of a city at night—

so that you and I must carry our practice, flickering in wind,
toward one another? *Too many facts assumes the appearance of none:*

as in Times Square or Tsim Sha Tsui: *the moreness ascends
inevitably to a threshold.* At the intersection a man jingles

in his hand the phrase *I don't love you.*
If, as Zong Bing believed, gazing at a painted mountain

is the same as traveling to the mountain,
will I, by reading this scroll, converse with the night visitor?

Exile of language: the narrow place:
a whole book encased in a name. Can we bear it.

The seventy tongues at Sinai. The hubbub. Yet intelligible.
Do you remember the gold calf, how he hid his face.

Truth is a refrain. Into forty years of wilderness, Nachshon
walked ahead, seeking a word whose sum was ascent.

An act of naming: his question was affirmation. But yours
is a pilgrimage in ink. The light goes on speaking its slow letters

through the valley. Who are the bearers. The words you read are written
on a hand winding rope, winding as it withdraws.

Letter Spoken in Wind

Today we walked the inlet Nybøl Nor
       remembering how to tread on frozen snow.
             Ate cold sloeberries

that tasted of wind—a white pucker—
       spat their sour pits in snow. Along
             the horizon, a line of windmills dissolved

into white field. Your voice
       on the phone *a gesundt in dein keppel*
             you blessed my head. Six months now

since I've seen you. There are
       traces of you here, your curls still dark
             and long, your woven dove,

the room you stayed in: send your syllables,
       I am swimming below the tide-
             mark. Words shed overcoats, come

to me undressed, slender-limbed, they have no
       letters yet. It is the festival
             of lights, I have no

candles. I light one for each night,
       pray on a row
             of nine lighthouses.

As if with pollen, Jerusalem's air is saturated, its walls crammed with prayers. Mail carriers receive God's letters and packages daily. Each is opened and archived. Once a man wrote, *Dear God, all I need is 600 shekels for my operation, and I will live a healthy life again.* The postal workers took up a collection and gathered, one by one, two by two, 500 shekels, and sent them. Soon a second letter arrived: *Dear God, next time, please don't send help by post, because those thieving mailmen stole a hundred shekels from me.*

Invitations to the God

Missives buried or burned, set like mortar
in the wall: letter written in grease,
letter of the mute child, letter that leans

on one leg, the flammable letter, the letter
weighing seven stone. Letter whose eyes
cannot open in the face of love. Written in milk,

sculpted on a potter's wheel. Akin
to crow's feet, redolent of dreams,
of unpaid bills, in mid coitus. Letter

on its knees. The one that unfurls like an overcoat.
The one hoisted to warn others.
The one that waited for hours in the café

before leaving. Wrapped in umbilical cord.
That rises to its toes saying
holy, holy, holy. The one halted

by the arrival of the warden. The one in Orion.
Permeated with the odor of diesel, the conductor's whistle.
Letter charting the sun amid a flock of pigeons.

From the shunned mother. Letter encrusted
with snails. Composed with the left hand bound. Slipped
behind a girl's ear. Soaked three years in wine.

Of the flowered chupah, of the I-You. Arched
with laughter for three days. Arriving
like phosphorescence. Honeycombed

with hunger. Letter of ten thousand
masks, semaphores, sunken galleons,
ten thousands modes of beckoning.

Gematria

On the corner a father of two sons
asks me directions, but I
am too busy laundering the next day's sheets.

Having eaten a meal of the small hours,
my soul is an ant carrying the fist of her guilt.

The city keeps plucking out its memory
as it flees hysterically toward the future.

Off the metro a man named Tristeza follows me,

looking in each store window as I do, reading
book covers, eyeing pastries, a housewares shop
guarded by seven porcelain goddesses

standing on smiling fish—or, it is this woman,
who unbuttons, silently, her shirt—she has finally arrived
in a blue hat: *We are making something together*

in a dark room. One day we will see what we've done.

Yes, perhaps it is a woman off the metro.
Perhaps it is a collage that contains a live butterfly.

Squire the Hour

Squire my measure of skin, flesh the paseo
from bundle to fondle. Your hands will ring
in the hour, will dwell from tip to tip. Unscaffold.
Unstring. Bind conjugate leaves to spine. Fuse

the lambent day flush between us. Love recites this room
while a flung moment croons sotto voce, sotto
voce, venetian-blinds your relishing gesture,
resumes its caress. Resumes.

The *Dulce*

Amidst six-toed cats, eye-patched dogs, hucksters
peddling parrots and tankers, a chicken,

knife strapped to leg, said it knew the way back.
We were hardly ever sober but I am sure

it was there. There that you catamaraned
me on the centripetal key, while a pelican quoted the sea,

sailed its galleon belly. Past porches and rickshaws,
we perched by turns on the siesta rim, woken

by our bodies' calypso, *sweet lychee, sweet
lime*. Hammocked by the heat.

"Faith" is a fine invention
When Gentlemen can *see*—
But *Microscopes* are prudent
In an Emergency.

Emily Dickinson

Letter as an Ode
To FOXP2

Just the slip from no to yes: two molecules,
a gear and a lever, to grant the soul

its ventriloquy. To answer "Here I am."
Or not. I imagine the two motes nacre-backed,

clasped to a gene whose polyglot proteins
orchestrate the vibration of voice box.

For whose sake, this interrogation that begins at birth,
this long dialog with night? Cellular machinery

opened our mouths, let the blueprint replicate,
let it take its rise, so that now when you open

your lips, a thousand tongues soliloquize:
speak your self as god speaks you.

Eros

Célestine knew the stillness of sycamore was more divine
when flustered by wind. She led the other girls at night
to Saint Médard and in filmic delirium they consumed dirt

from the grave of François de Pâris. To choke full,
stem and root, supine, vulpine. Convulsionists, *sécouistes*
flocked to the miracle: girls trampled, pierced,

their scavenger exclamations. Were they the arrows of the Lord?
The tableau writhing. The script read *bring yourself closer
to his aphrodisiac silence.* Dead at thirty-six, the deacon

was buried with the poor. Célestine's eyes grew accustomed.
She was certain the image would emerge, as when the eyes fix
on the space a star is not.

River View of the Village: Across the water is a town known for its thistles and thatched roofs. When a woman gives birth there, her cousins gather in a circle around her and bless the newborn, saying, *May you not fool yourself, may you not fool God, and may you not fool other people.*

Skin of the Pear: Wall of iron enclosing the town.

Kavannah: Yoked like a set of buckets, two villages are linked by a bridge. The frozen path that the river becomes in January is *kavannah*. Inner direction is *kavannah*. The experience of two sorrows is *kavannah*.

In Gaitskill Bog

My father writes a eulogy he will never deliver.
The mother at his feet, hair as dark as years.
A younger brother lifts a window to step

into air, an older brother, darkening
as footprints do in snow, confides

In Gaitskill Bog it takes fifteen years

A brother who was not ready yet,
a brother who was broken open, shucked,
a meal of salt on a black plate.

In Gaitskill Bog it takes fifteen years

for a footprint to disappear.
My father attends a funeral never held,
scattering photographs into the Atlantic

from a boat that will not sail.
I would lay my arm across his shoulders
and say *Look here, they are handing out loaves*

at the door, fresh loaves.

Quietus

At the equator the purveyor of night travels
1,000 miles per hour, banks and yaws
toward its sprocket. While the body
incubates tautology, the mind

toboggans ahead. The latent emblem is shaped
by an instant of exposure—*tefillin,
mezuzah*, six words beginning *HEAR*.
After all, the French philosopher remarked,

*there is the living sound of wood
inside the mechanism*. Recite the alphabet
end to end until it ignites into prayer. In the shtetl
they knew it. And earlier, when gods amassed

like flies over sacrificial sheep. Forgive me,
gentle friend, but this is a catastrophe
that recurs: and I have a hard time
discerning figure from foreground.

... an endless exercise of preparation... for that final act of crossing the river, a step that is never taken.
Rabbi Arthur Green

Has a wooden house in Vilijampole. Is a house owner.
Russian revision list

The shadow on the balustrade, and the folded name frayed by each family member upon arrival at the island, is also *kavannah*.
Pamphlet of Useful Phrases

As Light Breaks

      you will be walking through an alley of sycamores.
It will all be right, you will understand
      the traffic, the woman throwing soda cans,
the crane over a wrecked building. The metro will move
      underground like blood in your veins,
you will read the pigeons' nervous bustle.
      You will see car tracks in snow, the dark
striations marking out a map. You will turn,
      you will not know the word for why.

Détrompe l'Oeil

The headless watchers turn their torsos west.
Dearest heuristic: to deny the existence of the picture plane.
See how the street retreats to a point—
how this length of cloth trails toward you—

would you ever guess each part is carved from a single block
of wood? Both the wetlands and the bluffs.
Curtain and rod, nude and frame. In the eye's corner
a mannequin shifts her weight, tucks back her hair.

A life that casts a shadow in imitation of a life suspended
from an actual hook. But the painted xenia is offered
with genuine hospitality—sympathetic chain
between the grapes of Zeuxis and the marauding crows.

The oak leaves are as scarlet as today: the ebb of chlorophyll
is what draws the curtain. And when fire filters through the pupil,
reflections are more than mimesis. The eye is water,

the eye is fire. What comprehension of the human circumstance,
the temptation for the hand. Giotto's surreptitious flies
resting on saints' robes, Pistoletto's mirrored easel—

I struggle to distinguish between canvas and field
beyond the window. When I press against the glass,
I am not sure the cedars do not press back.

Pilgrim Road

I am chasing a bus on a Texas road named for the Virgin,
my dress like a poppy.

Some days it is this way: a father puts some fish
on his daughter's plate because a woman

sitting on the curb looks up to see another woman
on a bicycle; in the Latvian fortune teller's hallway,

someone plays drums while she reads the cards
and through the half-open door her husband

puts on a pair of pants, walks across the room,
tucking in his shirt. *Soul is a flute*, she says, touching

my chest. Fingers writing about fingers.
She with three children and one suitcase, where is the train,

the sandwiches and tea. There, a boy kisses a girl
goodbye and runs to join his lover, who swells

with waiting. Where did I misplace the story in my fist?
Narrow traffic lanes, past the train station steps covered

with squatters and dogs, past the sex shop,
its long mirrors, man smoking in the doorway,

Slavic crêpe-maker with his knowing eye
eating rapidly at lunchtime. A woman asks

How did I get here, looking at her watch again.
My heart turns over, a child sweating at night.

I've been looking for a word for days—not in the sand
in my slipper, not in the dream of losing a cat.

Thoughts you can slice your finger on—
a swarm of sirens wakes me after midnight,

someone in my bed. Arm in arm with myself
I leave the eighth floor, its enormous window,

the view of the Pantheon, and walk diagonally
through the city, following first this stranger, then that.

A zigzag of scooters, old men toss *boules*
amidst ponies and sycamores. In the public garden

girls traverse a cloth world in sock feet
while miniature boats spin toward each other.

At five a.m. a woman wakes her children
to see Paris's first snow, quivers

of breath shot in the flickering air.
Later there will be constellations in their hair,

blessed children eating their breakfast with jam.
Go, she says. *Pour your palmful of water*

from one hand to the other. This morning
I peel off fresh dreams like stamps.

Acknowledgments

Grateful acknowledgment is made to the editors of the publications in which these poems first appeared, a few in earlier versions or under different titles.

Borderlands, "The Baker Folds What He Does Not Remember,"
    "In Gaitskill Bog"
Gulf Coast, "In Cambium Lucida"
Helen Burns Poetry Anthology: New Voices from the Academy of American Poets' University & College Prizes, 1999–2008, edited by Mark Doty, "Letter Spoken in Wind"
Innisfree Poetry Journal, "Traveling Peddler's Declaration," "Eros," "In the Loire Valley," "After the Eclipse: Village Riddle," "Village of Twice-Salted Seas"
In Posse Review, "As Light Breaks," "Looking for Hibiscus"
Nimrod: International Journal of Poetry and Prose, "Letter Spoken in Wind"
Spinning Jenny, "Gematria"
The Academy of American Poets, Inc., "Village of Pulleys and Locomotion"

Notes

"*Consult these photographs...*" In Jewish folklore, a *dybbuk* is a restless spirit that may inhabit a person to accomplish a task. In a nineteenth-century tale, a rabbi tells a young girl possessed by a dybbuk to carry a wind-up alarm clock and that when it rings at 4:30, the dybbuk will be exorcised. At the stroke of 4:30, the bell rings, the girl jumps, and the dybbuk flees. (It is noteworthy that the first mechanical alarm clock was invented in 1787 by Levi Hutchins of Concord, NH, and was built to ring only at 4:00 a.m., when Mr. Hutchins had to wake up for work.)

"In Cambium Lucida" is for Jens.

"*Enter the region from the northwest...*" refers to Rochester, NY.

"When All Speech Has Ceased Within" is for G.C. Waldrep, and refers to his poem "Varieties of Religious Experience" (*Goldbeater's Skin*, 2003). Stanza seven borrows a phrase from an article written by Thomas de Zengotita.

Stanza seven of "Gematria" borrows from Arthur Miller's *Timebends*.

"Letter as an Ode" is dedicated to FOXP2, the gene responsible for language ability. The human FOXP2 differs from that of the chimpanzee by two molecules, the mouse by three, the zebra finch by seven, and the Neanderthal by zero.

The Yiddish epigraph is borrowed from the front page of a nineteenth-century chapbook. I would like to thank my grandparents for its accuracy.

"After the Eclipse: Village Riddle" and "After the Eclipse: Village Tale" are for Ilya Kaminsky.

The epigraph from Edmond Jabès is taken from Rosemarie Waldrop's translation of *Book of Questions*, Volume II, and appears courtesy of Wesleyan University Press.

The third stanza of "Quietus" paraphrases a line from Roland Barthes' *Camera Lucida*.

Rabbi Arthur Green's words from *Seek My Face, Speak My Name* (Northville, NJ: Jason Aronson, 1992) appear with the author's kind permission.

Thanks to Herbert Neumann for the gracious permission to reproduce Francis Picabia's "Parade amoureuse, 1917" on the cover. Thanks to the MOMA and the National Gallery of Art.

Many thanks to the Virginia Center for the Creative Arts and Hedgebrook. Thanks to the editors of Black Lawrence Press, Colleen Ryor and Diane Goettel, Steven Seighman, and Dzanc Books. Heartfelt thanks to Craig Arnold, J.K. Barret, Frank Bidart, Camille Bloomfield, K. Bradford, Mariana Di Cio, Kate Dufresne, Roland Flint, Sarah Hannah, Kurt Heinzelman, Susan Howe, Ilya Kaminsky, Josh Keller, Caroline Kim, August Kleinzahler, Jens Klenner, Tina Pamintuan, Steve Sapienza, Will Schroeder, Mathias Svalina, Arthur Sze, Caroline Vuillemin, G.C. Waldrep, David Wevill, Debra Weintraub, and my family.

Rachel Galvin's poems and translations appear in journals including *Drunken Boat, Gulf Coast, McSweeneys,* and *The Academy of American Poets, Inc.* She is the author of a chapbook of poems, *Zoetrope* (2006).